# The Beautiful Book for

# REBELS

Laine Cunningham

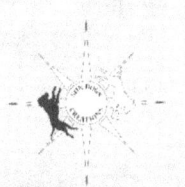

The Beautiful Book for Rebels

Published by Sun Dogs Creations
*Changing the World One Book at a Time*

Print ISBN: 9781946732729

Cover Design by Angel Leya

Copyright © 2018 and 2019 Laine Cunningham

All rights reserved. No part of this book may be reproduced in any form or by any means, electronic, mechanical, digital, photocopying or recording, except for the inclusion in a review, without permission in writing from the publisher.

The

# BEAUTIFUL

# BOOK

# SERIES

Align Your Passion With Your Purpose

REGRET ONLY

WHAT YOU LEAVE UNDONE.

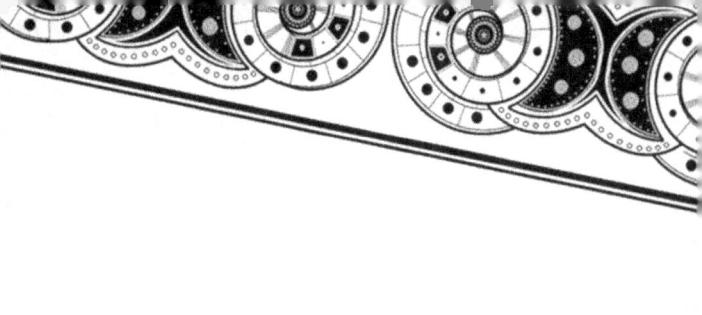

A DIFFICULT DAY MAKES

TOMORROW EVEN BETTER.

Myths are true for those who believe.

THE EDGE OF THE CLIFF OFFERS THE BEST VIEW.

Under pressure, common silica becomes precious opal.

A CRYSTAL'S STRUCTURE EXTENDS IN ALL DIRECTIONS.

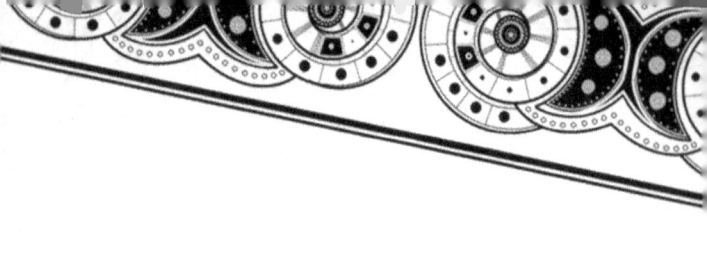

Boundaries are valid

only if

you agree

to be bound.

ABIDE BY

YOUR OWN RULES

RATHER THAN

THE RULES OF OTHERS.

WHEN THE ROAD TURNS ROUGH, GROW WINGS AND FLY.

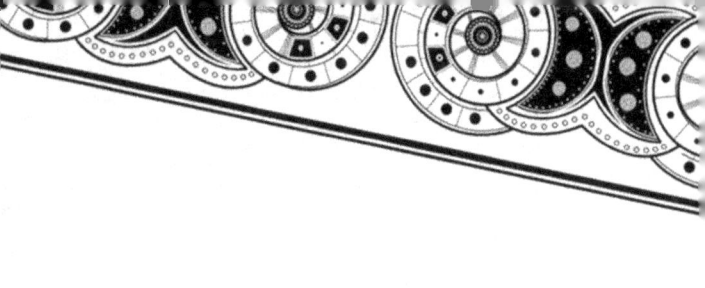

THE DEFINITION OF SUCCESS

IS SUBJECT TO CHANGE.

An outpost is often the best command post.

Strong wills develop strategic skills.

Mountains arise

from unseen forces.

Move past the insignificant to reveal the significant.

Volcanic activity

alters the landscape.

IF YOUR SHIP

SPRINGS A LEAK,

LEARN HOW TO SWIM.

One plant can seed an entire meadow.

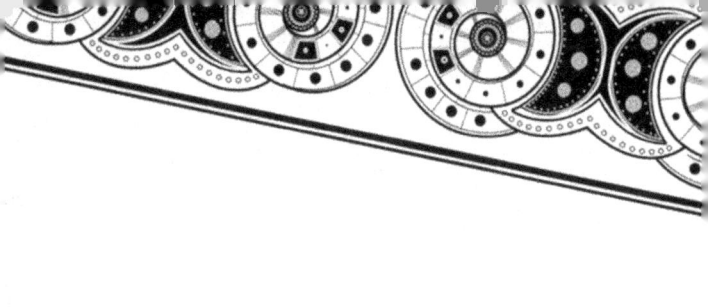

COMPETITION ENHANCES

INDIVIDUAL VOLITION.

A BIRD IN FLIGHT CAN PICK ITS ALTITUDE.

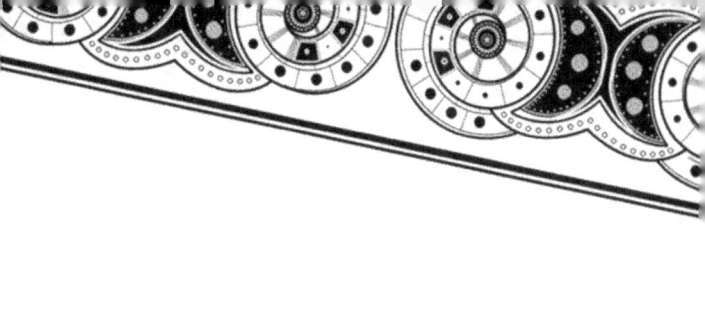

Stopping short can be as important as leaping first.

Many crops grow

in shallow furrows.

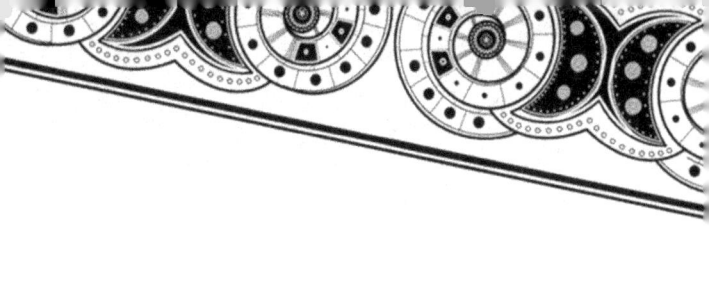

The oak that

stands alone

grows the longest limbs.

Resilience is earned as much as learned.

GRIT IS A

UNIVERSAL PASSPORT.

THOSE WHO SURVIVE

WILL EVENTUALLY THRIVE.

THE ENTIRE UNIVERSE

SPRANG FROM A VOID.

THE UNBLINKING EYE

PIERCES THE FOG.

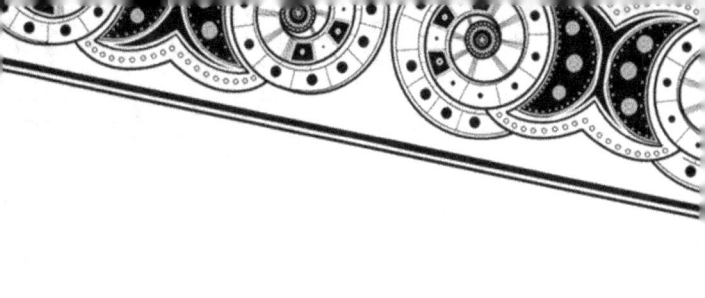

THE TRAIN THAT LEAVES

WITHOUT YOU

WAS NOT THE

RIGHT TRAIN.

Winning by a nose

is as victorious

as winning by a length.

Forget sink or swim.

Just float.

A HARD RAIN REPLENISHES

THE FERTILE SOIL.

The taste for adventure savors many flavors.

Find your own rhythm

to set your own beat.

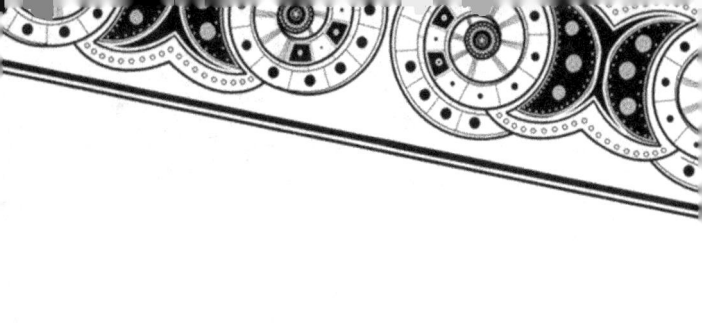

Artistry is not confined to the artist.

Logic is best tempered with intuition.

Curiosity is creativity's

lifelong partner

A DAILY ROUTINE IS THE LINCHPIN OF INSIGHT.

Mud pies are messy and a hell of a lot of fun.

Escape velocities

are different

on different planets.

Know which rules to break and which to adjust.

Rebels know

when to stand firm.

Outliers command

A different perspective.

Time does not pass equally at all locations.

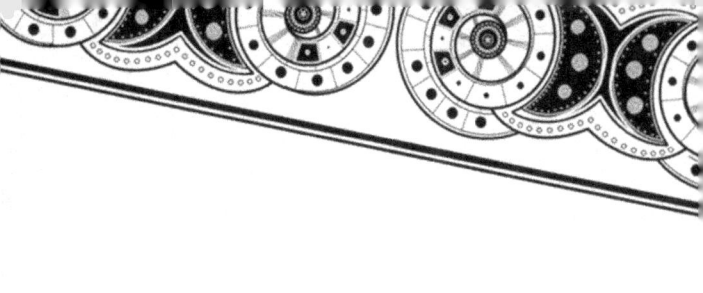

Breaking useless rules makes other rules more useful.

One quiet word

shatters

oppressive silence.

A COMPASS CALIBRATED WITH ETHICS IS ENDLESSLY RELIABLE.

Tribulation can be the gateway to triumph.

What others fear

to attempt

might simply require

more effort.

Persistence transforms mistakes into a process of elimination.

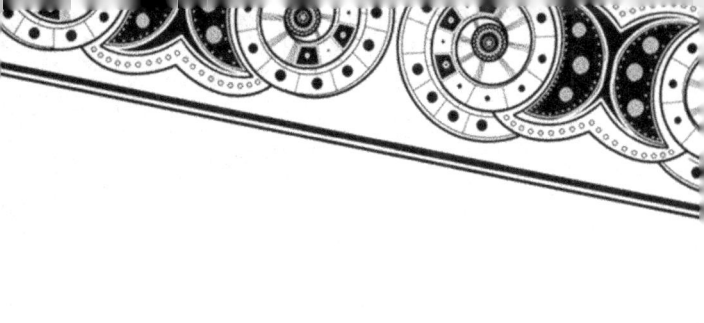

THERE IS ALWAYS

A BETTER WAY.

Boldness blends visionary thinking with the courage to act.

The flame of inspiration melts all resistance.

There are no rules

except

those you choose

to follow.

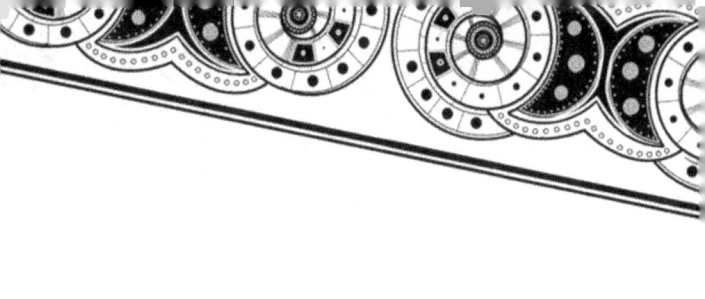

When you travel deep into space, you will lose sight of Earth.

Rule breakers are success makers.

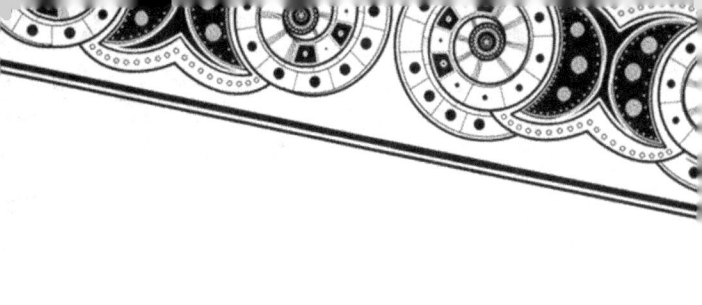

Boundaries are most in need of exploration.

Forward is not

the only direction.

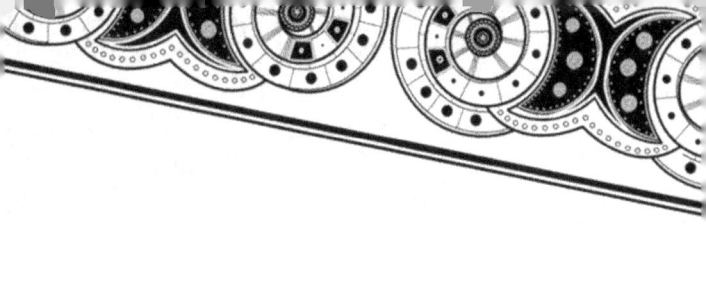

The impossible is only impossible now.

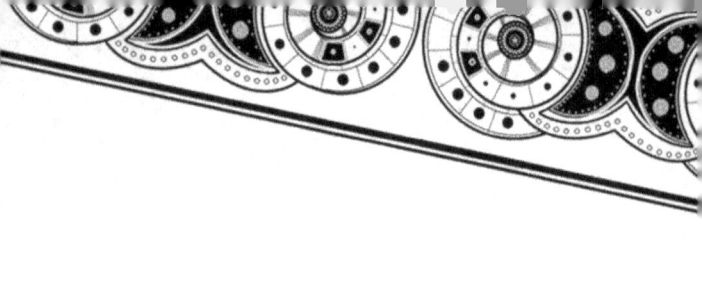

Improbable is not the same as impossible.

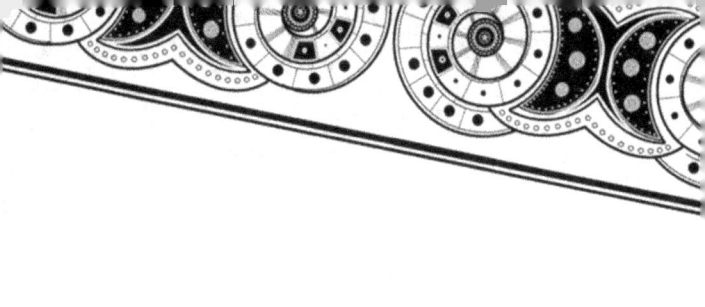

Luck yields only what you have sown.

You need not own

a fortune

to be fortunate.

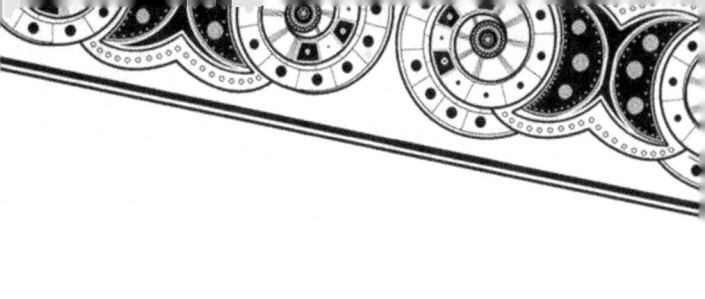

ELUSIVE ANSWERS

ARE REVEALED

WHEN YOU ASK

A DIFFERENT QUESTION.

The process of discovery

is also

the process of invention.

HARNESS THE ABUNDANT

TO LOCATE THE SCARCE.

Follow the lodestar
even if
only you can see it.

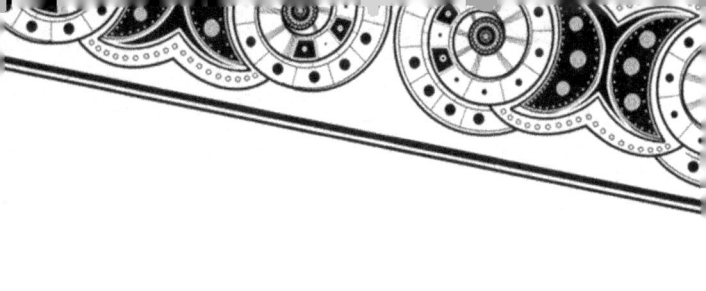

History is made by those who are both bold and thoughtful.

Clamp down and never let go.

## NOVELS BY LAINE CUNNINGHAM

*The Family Made of Dust*

*Beloved*

*Reparation*

## OTHER BOOKS BY LAINE CUNNINGHAM

*Woman Alone: A Six-Month Journey Through the Australian Outback*

*On the Wallaby Track*

*Seven Sisters: Spiritual Messages from Aboriginal Australia*

*Writing While Female or Black or Gay*

*The Zen of Travel*
*The Zen of Gardening*
*Zen in the Stable*
*The Zen of Chocolate*
*The Zen of Dogs*

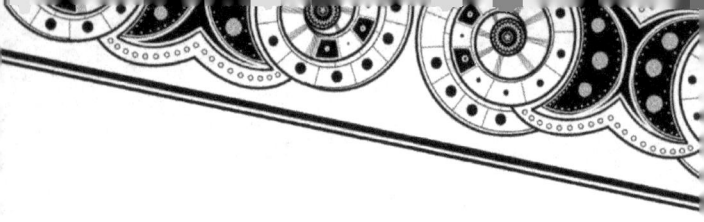

*The Wisdom of Puppies*
*The Wisdom of Babies*
*The Wisdom of Weddings*

*Bikes of Berlin*
*Necropolises of New Orleans I & II*
*Ruins of Rome I & II*
*Ancients of Assisi I & II*
*Panoramas of Portugal*
*Nuances of New York*
*Glimpses of Germany*
*Impressions of Italy*
*Altitudes of the Alps*
*Knights Through the Ages*
*Coast of California*
*Utopia of the Unicorn*
*Flourishes of France*
*Portraits of Paris*
*Tableaus of Tbilisi*
*Grandeur in the Republic of Georgia*

*The Beautiful Book of Questions*
*The Beautiful Book for Dream Seekers*
*The Beautiful Book for Rebels*
*The Beautiful Book for Women*
*The Beautiful Book for Lovers*

www.ingramcontent.com/pod-product-compliance
Lightning Source LLC
Chambersburg PA
CBHW071755080526
44588CB00013B/2246